WORDS ARE POWERFUL
CHOOSE THEM WISELY

KIND WORDS ARE LIKE HONEY

SWEET TO THE SOUL AND
HEALTHY FOR THE BODY.

PROVERBS 16:24 (NLT)

ISBN: 978-1-7371659-0-3
First Edition May 2021
Words are like Honey : Bee Brave
All rights reserved.

WordsLikeHoney.com

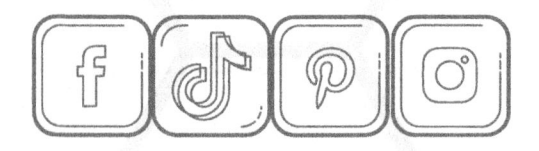

Dedicated with love
to my remarkable father,
Dr. Bill Ross.
He is the reason I adore
words, write every day
and collect quotes.
I love you Dad!

Laurie Allen

Courage is grace under pressure.

- EARNEST HEMINGWAY

It takes courage to grow and become who you really are.

- E.E. CUMMINGS

Above all, be the heroine of your life, not the victim.

- NORA EPHRON

You know, sometimes all you need is twenty seconds of insane courage. Just literally twenty seconds of embarrassing bravery. And I promise something great will come of it.

— BENJAMIN MEE,
WE BOUGHT A ZOO

Be brave and fearless to know that even if you do make a wrong decision, you're making it for good reason.

- ADELE

You cannot swim for new horizons until you have the courage to lose sight of the shore.

- WILLIAM FAULKNER

Believe in yourself. You are braver than you think, more talented than you know and capable than more than you imagine.

- ROY T. BENNETT

The most
courageous act
is to still think
for yourself.
Aloud.

- COCO CHANEL

Have enough courage to trust love one more time and always one more time.

- MAYA ANGELOU

I hope you live a life you're proud of. If you find you're not,
I hope you have the courage to start all over again.

- ERIC ROTH

Freedom lies in being bold.

- ROBERT FROST

> To a brave man, good and bad luck are like his left and right hand. He uses both.
>
> — ST. CATHERINE OF SIENA

Being brave means knowing that when you fail, you don't fail forever.

- LANA DEL RAY

Fortune always favors the brave.

- P.T. BARNUM

Courage is found in unlikely places.

- J.R.R. TOLKIEN

Scared is what you're feeling. Brave is what you're doing.

- EMMA DONOGHUE, *ROOM*

You can chose courage or you can choose comfort, but you cannot choose both.

- BRENÉ BROWN

Courage is being scared to death but saddling up anyway.

- JOHN WAYNE

You can't be brave if you've only have had wonderful things happen to you.

- MARY TYLER MOORE

Have the courage to follow your heart and intuition. They somehow already know what you truly want to become.

- STEVE JOBS

If people are
doubting how far
you can go,
go so far you can't
hear them.

- MICHELE RUIZ

If you can't fly,
then run.
If you can't run,
then walk.
and if you can't
walk, then crawl
but whatever you
do you have to
keep moving.

- MARTIN LUTHER KING JR

Courage is contagious. When a brave man takes a stand, the spines of others are often stiffened.

- BILLY GRAHAM

If you dream it, you can do it.

- WALT DISNEY

You get in life what you have the courage to ask for.

- OPRAH WINFREY

Our greatest weakness lies in giving up. The most certain way to succeed is to always try one more time.

- THOMAS EDISON

Only those who risk going too far can possibly find out how far one can go.

- T.S. ELIOT

Bravery is not the quality of the body. It is of the soul.

- MAHATMA GANDHI

For God has not given us a spirit of fear and timidity, but of power, love and self-discipline.

- 2 TIMOTHY 1:7

Have I not commanded you? Be strong and courageous Do not be afraid; do not be discouraged, for the Lord your God will be with you wherever you go.

- JOSHUA 1:9 NIV

Second chances aren't rare; however, to take them requires extraordinary courage.
Be brave enough to embrace a returned opportunity.

- LAURIE ALLEN

Courage is fear
that has said
its prayers.

- DOROTHY BERNARD

Courage is simply not one of the virtues, but the form of every virtue at the testing point.

- C.S. LEWIS

In order to achieve anything, you must be brave enough to fail.

- KIRK DOUGLAS

Success is not final; failure is not fatal. It is the courage to continue that counts.

- WINSTON CHURCHILL

If you are lucky enough to find a way of life you love, you have to find the courage to live it.

- JOHN IRVING

Do not be afraid;
just believe.

- MARK 5:36 NIV

Failure is often life's greatest teacher, so fail often and fail forward.

- GARY KELLER

Never say never, because limits, like fears, are often just an illusion.

- MICHAEL JORDAN

To be courageous requires no exceptional qualifications, no magic formula, no special combination of time, place, and circumstance. It is an opportunity that sooner or later is presented to us all.

- JOHN F. KENNEDY

Be on your guard; stand firm in the faith; be courageous; be strong. Do everything in love.

- 1 CORINTHIANS 16:13-14 NIV

To uncover your true potential you must first find your own limits and then have to courage to blow past them.

- PICABO STREET

The kind of beauty I want most is the hard-to-get kind that comes from within – strength, courage, dignity.

- RUBY DEE

You miss 100 percent of the shots you don't take.

- WAYNE GRETZKY

Kind heart,
fierce mind,
brave spirit.

- ANONYMOUS

A strong person is not the one who doesn't cry. A strong person is the one who is quiet and sheds a tear for a moment, and then picks up her sword and fights again.

- ANONYMOUS

I want to see you
be brave.

- SARA BARILLES

I want a courageous heart, a heart that does the right thing even when it's afraid.

- LAUREN GASKILL

When you are in doubt, be still, and wait; when doubt no longer exists for you, then go forward with courage.

- CHIEF WHITE EAGLE

Do not fear,
for I am with you.

- ISAIAH 4:10 NIV

Courage is the mistress and queen of all virtues.

- LATIN PROVERB

Today walk by courage in all that you do.

— HEATHER STILLULYEN

If you are ever afraid of anything, do not deny it, but behave as if you feared nothing.

- ANNA LEE WALDO, *SACAJAWEA*

Where there's hope, there's life. It fills us with fresh courage and makes us strong again.

— ANNE FRANK

Be on your guard;
stand firm in faith;
be courageous;
be strong.

- 1 CORINTHIANS 16:13
NIV

There may be people that have more talent than you, but there's no excuse for anyone to work harder than you.

- DEREK JETER

With enough courage, you can do without a reputation.

- RHETT BUTLER,
GONE WITH THE WIND

Heroes may not be braver than anyone else. They're just braver five minutes longer.

- RONALD REAGAN

Courage, dear heart.

- C.S. LEWIS

Made in the USA
Las Vegas, NV
28 May 2021